AF477044

PORTRAIT OF GLAMORGAN

NICK JENKINS

HALSGROVE

First published in Great Britain in 2008

Title page photograph: **Limestone beach near Nash Point**

British Library Cataloguing-in-Publication Data
A CIP record for this title is available from the British Library

ISBN 978 1 84114 817 5

Halsgrove House
Ryelands Industrial Estate, Bagley Road,
Wellington, Somerset TA21 9PZ
Tel: 01823 653777
Fax: 01823 216796
email: sales@halsgrove.com
website: www.halsgrove.com

Printed and bound by Grafiche Flaminia, Italy

Introduction

Back in 1974, as part of the Local Government re-organisation Act of 1972, the county of
Glamorgan disappeared, to be replaced by West Glamorgan, Mid Glamorgan and South
Glamorgan. This came as both a bit of a shock and a disappointment to many who considered them-
selves to be 'of and from Glamorgan'; all the more so as Glamorgan as a county had been in existence since the tenth century, originally under the name of Morgannwg. If this wasn't enough of a
shock to the system, along came another raft of legislation, doing away with the three counties and
replacing them with unitary authorities, in 1994. The only reference to the name Glamorgan is in the
Vale of Glamorgan Borough Council. A sad end to what was once a proud Welsh kingdom. But to
many folk, Glamorgan is still very much in existence, in mind if not in body.

However, the focus of this book is on the 'old' county of Glamorgan, stretching from Carmarthenshire
in the west to Breconshire (Powys) in the north, to Monmouthshire in the east, and the Bristol Channel
to the south. Of all the counties of Wales, none are as diverse in their landscape as Glamorgan. The
north of the county was the home of the Welsh coalfields; the Rhondda, Cynon, Taff, Ogmore and
Garw valleys, with their coal mines and supporting washeries, later to be replaced by light industry,
such as electronics factories and car component manufacturing. Similarly, the west of the county, with
the major exception of the Gower peninsula, was inclined towards industry. The two cities of Cardiff
and Swansea are major centres of welsh population and administration. By contrast the south of the
county was labelled as the Garden of Wales and the Garden of Cardiff, farming being the dominant
occupation, albeit tourism is starting to take off under a set of recently launched initiatives. Indeed,
these initiatives also cover the Rhondda and other valleys, well demonstrated by the setting up of the
popular Heritage Centre at Porth, portraying (and, indeed, celebrating) the life and culture of the
mining communities, where South Wales once ruled supreme.

To try and reflect this amazing diversity my photographic forays around Glamorgan took me to deep
valleys, high uplands, wooded waterfall gorges, long, sandy beaches, towering limestone cliffs and

wide open plains. I visited ancient churches, historic castles and all manner of archaeology and architecture in between. It is true that many of the sites I photographed were reasonably well known to me but it is also true that I discovered locations I had never even heard of, let alone visited. For example, I had no idea that the uplands of Mynydd y Gwair existed. This relatively quiet area is, and has been for some time, under the threat of an enormous wind farm development. Many folk have been actively involved in seeking to prevent this from happening, and it has featured in the media on a number of occasions. It is only about 40 miles from where I live and I had absolutely no idea it was there. However well one thinks one knows a location there are always surprises, and usually pleasantly surprising ones too!

I have presented my Portrait from the west of Glamorgan across to the east. We will start near the Carmarthenshire border, make our way round Gower, Swansea and Port Talbot, then around the valleys before coming down to the coast and into Cardiff. Inevitably, with a project of this size, and given the incredible variety and number of attractive locations in Glamorgan, I will have omitted some that may be your favourite spots. If this is the case I apologise but I do hope you will enjoy the pictures I have included as being representative of my home county! Mine was a journey full of delights and it seeks to prove the point that Glamorgan is truly an area rich in diversity, from the point of view of its inhabitants, its landscapes and its architecture. Join me as I present you with my Portrait of Glamorgan.

Nick Jenkins
2008

BRECON BEACONS NATIONAL PARK
CARMARTHENSHIRE
MONMOUTHSHIRE
Merthyr Tydfil
Mynydd y Gwair
AFAN VALLEY
RHONDDA VALLEY
Swansea
GOWER
Margam
Maesteg
Pontypridd
Rhossili
Caerphilly
Port Eynon
Kenfig
Porthcawl
Cowbridge
CARDIFF
Penarth
GLAMORGAN
NASH POINT HERITAGE COAST

Acknowledgements

Once again I owe a huge debt of thanks to my wife Anne and son Stephen for putting up with my absences as I traipsed all over the place, seeking out new locations and new angles on old locations.

I am also grateful to the team at Halsgrove for giving me the opportunity to once again show off the beauty of my home country of Wales. Not forgetting the patience of Karen Binaccioni who I succeeded in confusing utterly, and not just once!

St Cadoc's church, Cheriton
This is just one of several beautiful old churches on the Gower peninsula.

King Arthur's Stone, Cefn Bryn
High on the Cefn Bryn ridge, the capstone of this neolithic burial chamber was said to be a pebble thrown by King Arthur from his shoe whilst passing Carmarthen.

'Welcome to Town' Restaurant, Llanrhidian
Now considered a fine restaurant by many, this was once the village pub.

Upper standing stone, Llanrhidian
*The remains of an old Celtic cross, this 'standing stone'
has guarded the gateway to Llanrhidian church for very
many years.*

Oxwich Bay
A very popular beach and holiday resort seen from the Great Tor. I spent many happy days exploring here when I was growing up.

Port Eynon beach
Another of Gower's many large sandy bays, ever popular with holiday-makers.

Lifeboat Memorial, Port Eynon
Just inside the churchyard of St Cattwg this memorial is to three lifeboatmen drowned whilst attempting a rescue in 1916.

Gower Coast near Fall Bay
*Gower has a truly stunning coastline, comprised mainly of limestone cliffs and sandy bays.
The walk along the cliff tops is magnificent at any time of year.*

Rhossili Bay
Possibly the best known stretch of sand in Wales, Rhossili Bay forms the most westerly part of the Gower peninsula and to walk it from end to end is no mean feat.

Coastguard lookout hut
*I had gone to photograph the sun setting over Worm's Head on this evening,
but was immediately drawn to the scene of the coastguard locking up ready to go home.*

Whitford Sands
The sands, Gower's most northerly beach, front a large area of sand dunes and pine woods.
At the westerly end of the beach is an old disused cast iron lighthouse, the only one left in the UK
surrounded by sea (when the tide's in).

Sunset over Worm's Head
*This is the spot to come to for sunsets and big skies.
The Worm, or Wurm in norse, is a spectacular 'end' to
the Gower peninsula.*

Swansea Marina

The marina development has brought much needed business and accommodation to this part of the old Swansea Docks.

Swansea Marina and moored yachts
The marina is immensely popular with yachtsmen from far and wide and is invariably packed from end to end with masts.

Swansea Seafront
*The seafront is a popular promenade with locals and tourists alike, stretching from the marina across
Swansea Bay to Mumbles.*

Opposite: **Swansea Marina on a summer evening**
The evening sun caught this boat beautifully before it dipped below the buildings.

Statue of Dylan Thomas
The memory of this famous welsh poet and writer with his strong links to Swansea is celebrated in this statue by the marina.

Opposite: **Barn Mynydd y Gwair**
As often happens when I explore, I had no idea that Mynydd y Gwair even existed, let alone where it could be! It is a little known and hilly wilderness just north of Swansea and amply repaid some further investigation

Lliw Valley woodland
*One of several valleys running north/
south in the Mynydd y Gwair area.*

Opposite: **Upper Lliw Valley Reservoir**
*At the top of the Upper Lliw Valley,
and accessible only on foot, this
secluded reservoir is surrounded
by wooded hills.*

Melincourt Falls, Vale of Neath
These falls, near Resolven, drop eighty feet onto a pile of rocks – dramatic and always worth a visit.

Melincourt Falls – close up
The size of the rocks at the base of the falls is immense. I love the way the water sprays from boulder to boulder.

**Sgwd Gwladys Falls,
Vale of Neath**

*Gwladys was one of the many daughters
of King Brychan of Brycheiniog. Situated
on the River Pyrddin, this is probably my
favourite Welsh waterfall.*

Sgwd Gwladys Falls
Photographed from the top of the falls, reached easily up a short rocky scramble.

Goytre Valley
Running north from Port Talbot, this secluded agricultural valley is yet another of Glamorgan's less well publicised gems.

Margam House
You could spend a day on the Margam estate and only really discover half of it. Margam House is the old home of the Mansel, and latterly, Mansel Talbot, family. It is now in the care of Neath Port Talbot Borough Council.

Margam Abbey Chapter House
This wonderful old abbey was a Cistercian house, but met its fate at the Dissolution of the Monasteries in the sixteenth century.

Opposite: **Margam Abbey window arch**
Showing a detail of the fine architecture of this old abbey with the outlying abbey chapel of St Mary on the Hill 'through the window'.

Margam Orangery
This magnificent eighteenth century orangery is believed to be the longest in Britain.

Kenfig Pool
A natural pool, very popular with bird watchers.
It is said the lost city of Kenfig (Cynffig, in Welsh) lies buried beneath its waters.

Porthcawl Seafront
Winter brings a bleak ruggedness to the front at Porthcawl which in summer seems less harsh.

Rest Bay, Porthcawl
This wide sandy beach, just to the west of Porthcawl, is a Mecca for swimmers and surfers.

Opposite: **Old Lighthouse, Porthcawl**
Built in 1860, this old lighthouse on the breakwater was once gas powered.
In the background is a stretch of the Glamorgan Heritage Coast.

Cymmer Village
One of a number of old mining villages in the Afan Valley, Cymmer is a real joy to discover with its windy lanes, houses so closely built together and enormous chapel overlooking the tightly knit community.

Hebron Chapel, Cymmer
'Chapel' was for many years, and indeed still is, the mainstay of village life (along with the rugby club) in the Glamorgan valleys. Sadly they are now far less frequently attended, and many have been converted into houses or flats.

Afon Corrwg, Cymmer
Cymmer (in welsh, Cymer) means the joining place of two rivers, the river here being the Afon Corrwg, which joins the Afon Afan just below this point.

Opposite: **Sunnyside Terrace, Cymmer**
Sitting just inside Cymmer, Sunnyside Terrace, in the background, is a scene so typical of the Afan Valley; rows of houses set amidst stunning hillside scenery.

Glyncorrwg
Hidden at the end of a deep forested valley, Glyncorrwg was once a very busy coal mining centre, but with the closing of the pits in the 1970s, it almost died. Today, Glyncorrwg is an important mountain biking centre in some superb forestry and mountain scenery.

Abergwynfi terraced cottages
I just love the way all these differently coloured terraced houses gently climb the hill like toys or a slightly surreal painting.
This scene is so typical of the Glamorgan valleys.

Nantyffyllon
When I went to school nearby we used to refer to this village as 'Nantyfurtheron' as it was just further on from Maesteg, in the Llynfi Valley. It was a very dark and muggy day when the sun suddenly shone for a few seconds on the village and I managed to grab the shot.

Tonna Road, Caerau
To me, the houses of Tonna Road sum up the archetypal row of a Welsh mining community.

Llangeinor Arms and parish church
Both the church and pub are situated on the crest of the hill between the Ogmore and Garw Valleys.
Now I understand the meaning of the phrase 'thirst after righteousness'!

Opposite: **Tondu Iron Works**
Bought from Sir William Price by the Brogden family in 1854, the ironworks have been described as the most complete Victorian works of their kind. They are now occupied by, amongst others, the Bridgend Young Archaeologists Club.

Rainbow over the Cynon Valley
I had left the car on the hill between the Rhondda and the Cynon Valleys and walked over to a nearby trig point. Suddenly the heavens opened and then, after about ten minutes, came this. Moral: always carry a camera!

Opposite: **Glamorgan sheep**
No photographic study of any part of Wales could be complete without a sheep! This one was in a field next to the Llangeinor Arms and followed me for ages – must have spotted my camera..

Pen Pych Waterfall
*The waterfall and forestry walks are all very easily accessible
from Blaencwm in Rhondda Fawr, and help to debunk the
myth that Rhondda is all soot and chimneys!*

Cwmparc Village
This is a typical row of terraced houses, found in so many of the valley communities, and gives tantalising hints as to the steepness of the surrounding hillsides.

Graig Fawr, Cwmparc
This dead end valley, near the top of the Rhondda Fawr Valley, once a very busy coal mining area and the site of the original Parc and Dare Mines, has now been completely landscaped. The underlying rock in this area is Pennant sandstone.

Opposite: **Road over the Bwlch Pass**
This is a typical winding descent into the Rhondda Valley and Cwmparc, hinting at the wildness of the terrain before it became so developed.

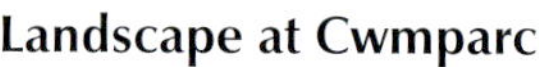

Landscape at Cwmparc
Once a landscape showing all the scars of extractive industry, Cwmparc is now surrounded by reclaimed land, with green commons and trees.

Nant y Gwyddon Picnic Site
Much of the Rhondda Valleys region is now being turned back to green; picnic sites, fishing pools and footpaths are becoming the norm and are proving very popular with locals and visitors alike.

Penrhys – Our Lady

Sitting 1100 feet above sea level, atop the ridge that divides the Rhondda Fawr (Great Rhondda) and Rhondda Fach (Little Rhondda), is the community of Penrhys, known for its links with history to beyond mediaeval times. The statue of Our Lady marks the site of an ancient chapel.

Looking across Pentre from Mynydd yr Eglwys
Rhododendrons cover the slopes of this green and fertile area – such a change from when 'coal was king'.

Ystrad, Rhondda
Viewed from the heights of Penrhys, Ystrad is typical of the long and narrow communities of the Rhondda Valleys.

Ferndale
Sitting in the Rhondda Fach Valley this former coal mining community once housed over 23,000 people per square mile, the highest density in Wales and England.

Opposite: **Partridge Road, LLwynypia**
Looking south down the Rhondda Fawr from Penrhys towards Llwynypia and showing the rows of houses snaking along the valley bottom.

Stanleytown
Nestling under the remains of the Wattsville Coal tip in the Rhondda Fach Valley, the neat rows of cottages seem to me to sum up all that is the Rhondda.

The Miner and His Wife, Tonypandy
Unveiled in 1993 by Viscount Tonypandy the statue was erected to commemorate the mining communities of the Rhondda Valleys.

The Pop Factory, Porth
*Once the home of the Corona soft drinks company, the Pop Factory is now a complex of studios covering
most TV and music recording requirements.*

Rhondda Heritage Park, Trehafod
Sited at the entrance to the Rhondda Valleys the Heritage Park is located in an old coal mine. It shows visitors just what a working mine was like and explains in words and pictures the community life and spirit of those who lived (and continue to live!) here.

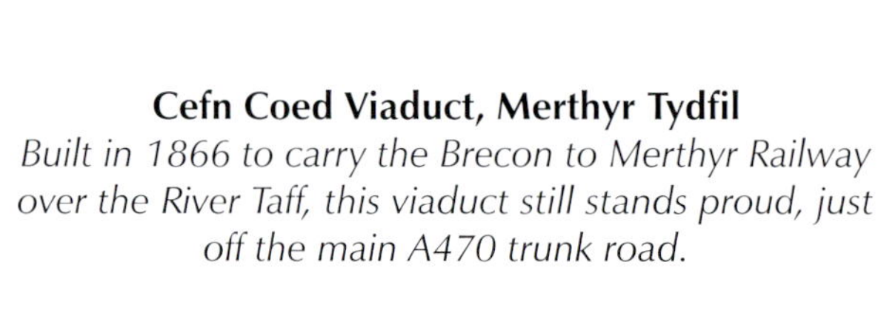

Cefn Coed Viaduct, Merthyr Tydfil
Built in 1866 to carry the Brecon to Merthyr Railway over the River Taff, this viaduct still stands proud, just off the main A470 trunk road.

Cyfarthfa Castle, Merthyr Tydfil
Built by the Crawshay family, ironmasters of Merthyr, Cyfarthfa Castle is linked to Rolf Harris, whose grandfather came from Merthyr, and houses one of his original paintings.

Opposite: **Rainbow over Pontypridd**
Rainbows often don't last too long so I screeched into a nearby car park and erected the tripod next to the car. And, yes, I did attract some funny looks!

The Old Bridge, Pontypridd
Built in 1756 by William Edwards, this was once the longest single-span bridge in Europe.

View from Ffordd y Bryniau
Looking south from the ridge of this ancient trackway shows the landscape so typical of the area between the fertile agricultural Vale and the harsher terrain of the Glamorgan valleys. This was shot near the village of Heol y Cyw.

Llantrisant parish church
Dedicated to the three Welsh saints Illtyd, Gwynno and Dyfodwg, the 'Church of the Three Saints' sits high on a hill next to the castle.

Llantrisant Castle
Little remains of this once strategically important castle, built in the thirteenth century by Richard de Clare.

Swan Street, Llantrisant
Once home to five pubs, this cobbled street is full of character.

Miskin parish church
St David's parish church was built around 1907, and replaced an old corrugated shed which had stood there for some thirty years. The Williams family of nearby Miskin Manor were largely responsible for its construction.

Holy Cross church, Cowbridge
Holy Cross church sits squarely in the middle of Cowbridge – access being via the north side from where this picture was taken.

Holy Cross church
View from the south side.

**West Door, Holy Cross church –
the Puzzle Lock**
*Whilst photographing the church I noticed
this intriguing lock surround fastened to
the west door.*

Opposite: **Holy Cross church – interior**
*The church of the Holy Cross has been a place
of worship for Cowbridge folk for a very long
time.*

Cowbridge town wall

Traces of this ancient wall surrounding the old town, in Welsh Bont Faen, can still be found. Completed in the thirteenth century there were four gates, the south gate still remaining.

Opposite and right: **Cowbridge Physic Garden**

This recent reconstruction of the 'Parterre' garden was completed in 2006. It replaces the old garden that was part of the Edmondes family residence from the eighteenth to the twentieth centuries.

Cowbridge Physic Garden
The garden has proved extremely popular with both locals and visitors. The building in the background is the old Cowbridge Grammar School, now private apartments.

'Vale of Glamorgan' pub, Cowbridge
One of a number of pubs along the main road through this quaint rural town.

Cowbridge War Memorial
Looking north towards the hills and valleys of Mid Glamorgan this monument, on Stalling Down, stands as a sentinel alongside an ancient roman road.

The Bush Inn, St Hilary
This quaint pub is not untypical of the Vale. St Hilary hit the news recently as being the first village in the UK with a road sign instructing SatNav users not to take the route advised – and risk getting lorries stuck in the narrow St Hilary lanes!

Opposite: **Llanblethian church – St John the Baptist**
There was a time when Cowbridge served as a chapel of ease for this fine church, built on a raised hill. Although seemingly overshadowed by Cowbridge, Llanblethian is a pretty village full of narrow, windy lanes.

Ogmore Castle
Situated on the River Ewenny, Ogmore Castle was built by William de Londres, a Norman knight, soon after 1100. The stepping stones lead to the tiny village of Merthyr Mawr.

Opposite: **Ewenny Priory**
Claimed by many to be the best example of a fortified Norman priory in Britain, this treasure lies hidden next to the Ewenny Brook.

Merthyr Mawr thatch
This idyllic village, with its thatched cottages and pretty church, lies just to the west of the Ogmore River south of Bridgend.

Candleston Castle
Buried amongst the dunes of Merthyr Mawr, Candleston Castle had finally to be abandoned due to the encroaching sand.

Pony trekking at Ogmore Castle
Pony trekking is very popular here, especially with the proximity of the wide sandy beach at Ogmore by Sea.

Opposite: **Glamorgan Heritage Coast at Southerndown**
The viewpoint near the old ruins of Dunraven Castle is superb, showing the nature of the limestone coast.
The best light is in the evening when the sun swings round to the west.

Nash Point

One of my favourite local spots, Nash Point is a place to recharge run-down batteries. The coastal scenery is dramatic, and it is possible to walk along the cliff tops in either direction.

Opposite: **Old Lighthouse, Nash Point**
There are two lighthouses here; this one, now defunct, and an operational one some 100 yards to the east. I was captivated by the light of the setting sun on the white wall, turning it orangey yellow.

Nash Point cliffs
The sunsets at Nash Point light up the Lias limestone cliffs to an almost fluorescent orange – this is a very popular spot with photographers and little wonder.

Beach at Nash Point
*The Glamorgan Heritage Coast is mostly made up of both Liassic and Carboniferous limestone,
the yellow cliffs being Lias.*

Opposite: **Sunset off Nash Point**
*The sunsets from this part of the Glamorgan Heritage Coast are truly spectacular, none more so
than this performance one recent February evening.*

Limestone beach near Nash Point
The Carboniferous limestone weathers into pavements and ledges of amazing patterns.

Llantwit Major beach
This apparent solitary rock is actually the end of a line of cliffs on the east side of Llantwit beach.

Opposite: **Moonrise over Somerset Farm, Marcross**
On my way home one evening after photographing at Nash Point I was captivated by the moody effect of this bright rising moon.

St Donat's Castle
Now home to 'The United World College of the Atlantic', this beautifully preserved castle on the Glamorgan Heritage Coast was once owned (and extensively restored) by the newspaper magnate William Randolph Hearst.

Beaupre Castle

Locally pronounced 'Bewper', this ruined castle near Cowbridge was once the home of the Bassett family of Glamorgan. The inside of the entrance is decorated with Doric, Ionic and Corinthian columns – a truly pretentious statement of wealth!

St Lythan's Burial Chamber, Wenvoe

It poured with rain when I arrived here, but after taking shelter under the capstone, I emerged to find some beautiful clean light.

Aberthaw Power Station
This enormous coal-fired edifice sits incongruously on the Glamorgan shoreline, on what was once the very busy little port of Aberthaw, known as the Leys.

Oilseed rape field near Cardiff International Airport
Across the road from the busy airport, this field might have been 1000 miles from anywhere.

Poppy flower
Growing along the edge of the rape field were these beautiful poppies by the dozen.

Barry Island
On one side of the Barry Island access road is a marina development, whilst on the other side is this large sandy beach with boats moored on the flats – such a contrast.

Barry Island beach
This large expanse of sand lies between Barry Island and the beach at Cold Knap.

Barry Island Harbour entrance

The entrance to this small harbour on the very end of Barry Island. Out in the Bristol Channel the islands of Flatholm, Steepholm and Lundy are clearly visible.

Barry Island Harbour and Bristol Channel
Showing the Bristol Channel, the Devon coast and one of many of the ships that navigate the Channel every day.

Penarth Pier

*One of only a handful of piers left in Wales, Penarth always draws me when I am out with the camera.
Opened in 1895, the pier has drawn thousands of visitors over the years.*

Penarth Pier Pavilion
Photographed from the beach the Pier Pavilion was added in 1926.

Opposite: **Daffodils – St Fagan's Museum of Welsh Life**
Springtime in this extremely popular open air museum celebrating Welsh culture, just to the west of Cardiff.

Cardiff Bay
*The Bay, still being developed, attracts many visitors, including the BBC's 'Dr. Who' and 'Torchwood'.
It started as a docks re-generation project and continues to grow, both upwards and outwards.*

Opposite: **Cardiff Bay 'Sails'**
The Sails on the Cardiff Bay barrage, with a strategically placed cloud!

Cardiff Civic Centre
Cardiff's magnificent Civic Centre, built around the turn of the twentieth century, is built largely of Portland stone, on land that was once owned by the Bute family.

Opposite: **Scott sculpture, Cardiff Bay**
Despite Scott's expedition to the South Pole being beaten by Roald Amundsen's Norwegian team, this has still been placed outside the Norwegian Church! No hard feelings then.

Roath Park Lake
Created by damming the Nant Fawr stream, this thirty acre lake is home to paddle boats, rowing boats and a large number of water birds, utterly indifferent to our waterborne pursuits.

Opposite: **Welsh National War Memorial**
This grand structure, initially built to celebrate the war dead of the First World War was commissioned in 1928.   It is surrounded by beautiful floral displays every year.

Roath Park 'Lighthouse'
*Not so much a lighthouse as a memorial to the ill-fated expedition to the South Pole by Captain Scott.
It was built in 1915 and is believed to be the only 'lighthouse' built in a lake!*

Opposite and overleaf: **Llandaff Cathedral**
*Built on an ancient site, the cathedral has had a troubled history, from being used as a
billet for Cromwell's troops to being blasted by a land mine. Still it stands proud, defying
all that history can throw at it.*

'Christ in Majesty'
*This enormous aluminium sculpture is the work
of the American Jacob Epstein and is the first
thing you see on entering the cathedral.*

Opposite: **Tinkinswood Burial Chamber**
*One of a number of such neolithic chambers in
the Vale of Glamorgan, Tinkinswood is believed
to have been built around 4000BC. Also known
as Castell Carreg, it lies just south of St Nicholas.
The capstone seen here weighs around 40 tons!*

Garth Hill from the Tumble
The Garth dominates the skyline north of Cardiff and is rich in ancient burial sites.

Opposite: **Castell Coch**
The 'Red Castle', built of red rubble sandstone, was designed by William Burges for the third Marquis of Bute, based on a French chateau. It sits on the foundations of a much earlier castle and is more of a folly. The first commercial vineyard in Britain once grew under its walls.

Castell Coch beech woods
*The trees growing on the slopes north of the castle are mainly beech,
and provide a superb backdrop the whole year round. Winter sun
catches the trunks well and lights up the dropped leaves.*

Caerphilly Castle
*It may not be commonly known that this massive
fortification is the second largest castle complex in
Britain, pipped to the post by Windsor Castle.*

Photographer's Notes

I am never too sure just how helpful it is to pore over the technology used to take my pictures, preferring instead to lay the main emphasis on the combination of a good pair of legs and a seeing eye. Nevertheless, the following is a short summary of how I approach my photography, and with what!

All the pictures in the book were taken either on a Nikon F5 film camera, using Fuji Velvia 50ASA slide film, or on a Nikon D2X digital camera, using Sandisk CF memory cards. Lenses (which are sometimes underused, at our peril) were all Nikon or Sigma, with focal lengths ranging from 17mm to 300mm. I invariably use a tripod; an excellent carbon fibre Gitzo generally, but on occasions where I want to get really close to a flower or similar I use a Uniloc tripod with a Benbo head. A spirit level gets my horizons nice and straight (yes, I know it is possible to do this in Photoshop or other post processing products.....don't get me started!!) as I try to place heavy emphasis on getting it right in the camera. I try and limit the use of filters, preferring to capture 'what is', but do make use of polarisers, and neutral density graduated filters to either even up the exposure if the sky is too bright or simply to enhance a stormy cloudscape.

I very often walk around an area before even taking my first shot, seeking out the most exciting angle and the best direction of the light. I will walk a complete 360 degree circle around an object before I photograph it, often to the amusement/amazement of passers by. And, after all that, I will probably discard the first 5 or so frames, until I find my rhythm.

The light? Well, sometimes I like to think I plan around it, but if the truth be told, it usually 'just happens'. Being there in the first place is, of course, the key. Photographers make their own luck.

In the end it's down to individual likes and dislikes. I do so hope you have enjoyed this portfolio of work – there were so many more I could have selected, but all things must draw to an end eventually.